100 INSPIRATIONAL QUOTES BY WINSTON CHURCHILL

QANA BOOKS

OTHER INSPIRATIONAL BOOKS IN THE SERIES:

100 Inspirational Quotes by Mark Twain
100 Inspirational Quotes by Mahatma Gandhi
100 Inspirational Quotes by Oscar Wilde
100 Inspirational Quotes by Friedrich Nietzsche
100 Inspirational Quotes by Confucius
100 Inspirational Quotes by Aristotle
100 Inspirational Quotes by Malcom X
100 Inspirational Quotes by Gautama Buddha
100 Inspirational Quotes by Ali ibn Abi Talib

WINSTON CHURCHILL

Winston Churchill was Prime Minister of the United Kingdom from 1940 to 1945, during the Second World War, and again from 1951 to 1955. Widely considered one of the 20th century's most significant figures, Churchill remains popular in the English-speaking world as one of the victorious wartime leaders who defended Europe against the spread of fascism.

His quotes and witticisms have become a mainstay of the English language and are often used in modern language.

If you're going through hell, keep going

Attitude is a little thing that makes a big difference

Courage is what it takes to stand up and speak; courage is also what it takes to sit down and listen

Never, never, never give up

We shall defend our island, whatever the cost may be, we shall fight on the beaches, we shall fight on the landing grounds, we shall fight in the fields and in the streets, we shall fight in the hills; we shall never surrender

The truth is incontrovertible. Malice may attack it, ignorance may deride it, but in the end, there it is

History will be kind to me for I intend to write it

12

To jaw-jaw is always better than to war-war

My most brilliant achievement was my ability to be able to persuade my wife to marry me

The pessimist sees difficulty in every opportunity. The optimist sees the opportunity in every difficulty

15

A fanatic is one who can't change his mind and won't change the subject

Solitary trees, if they grow at all, grow strong

We make a living by what we get,
but we make a life by what we give

The farther backward you can look,
the farther forward you can see

You have enemies? Good. That means you've stood up for something, sometime in your life

If we open a quarrel between past and present, we shall find that we have lost the future

21

History is written by the victors

Courage is rightly esteemed the first of human qualities because it is the quality which guarantees all others

Kites rise highest against the wind - not with it

24

An appeaser is one who feeds a crocodile, hoping it will eat him last

25

I never worry about action, but only inaction

26

A lie gets halfway around the world before the truth has a chance to get its pants on

We are masters of the unsaid words,
but slaves of those we let slip out

I am an optimist. It does not seem too much use being anything else

If you have an important point to make, don't try to be subtle or clever. Use a pile driver. Hit the point once. Then come back and hit it again. Then hit it a third time - a tremendous whack

Never hold discussions with the monkey when the organ grinder is in the room

31

The empires of the future are the empires of the mind

32

It is a good thing for an uneducated man to read books of quotations

Criticism may not be agreeable, but it is necessary. It fulfils the same function as pain in the human body. It calls attention to an unhealthy state of things

The best argument against democracy is a five-minute conversation with the average voter

35

Success consists of going from failure to failure without loss of enthusiasm

I am fond of pigs. Dogs look up to us. Cats look down on us. Pigs treat us as equals

All the great things are simple, and many can be expressed in a single word: freedom, justice, honor, duty, mercy, hope

38

The price of greatness is responsibility

Victory at all costs, victory in spite of all terror, victory however long and hard the road may be; for without victory, there is no survival

I am prepared to meet my maker. Whether my maker is prepared for the great ordeal of meeting me is another matter

We shape our buildings; thereafter they shape us

Play the game for more than you can afford to lose, only then will you learn the game

43

Let our advance worrying become advance thinking and planning

Mr. Attlee is a very modest man. Indeed he has a lot to be modest about

To build may have to be the slow and laborious task of years. To destroy can be the thoughtless act of a single day

It is always wise to look ahead, but difficult to look further than you can see

True genius resides in the capacity for evaluation of uncertain, hazardous, and conflicting information

One ought never to turn one's back on a threatened danger and try to run away from it. If you do that, you will double the danger. But if you meet it promptly and without flinching, you will reduce the danger by half. Never run away from anything. Never!

49

When you have to kill a man, it costs nothing to be polite

There is no such thing as public opinion. There is only published opinion

I am easily satisfied with the very best

52

Study history, study history. In history lies all the secrets of statecraft

It is a fine thing to be honest, but it is also very important to be right

54

Great and good are seldom the same man

55

It is more agreeable to have the power to give than to receive

Personally, I'm always ready to learn, although I do not always like being taught

57

We shall draw from the heart of suffering itself the means of inspiration and survival

There are a terrible lot of lies going about the world, and the worst of it is that half of them are true

It is a mistake to look too far ahead. Only one link of the chain of destiny can be handled at a time

Some people regard private enterprise as a predatory tiger to be shot. Others look on it as a cow they can milk. Not enough people see it as a healthy horse, pulling a sturdy wagon

61

Difficulties mastered are opportunities won

Never in the field of human conflict was so much owed by so many to so few

63

Everyone has his day and some days last longer than others

Perhaps it is better to be irresponsible and right, than to be responsible and wrong

65

A state of society where men may not speak their minds cannot long endure

If you have ten thousand regulations, you destroy all respect for the law

Too often the strong, silent man is silent only because he does not know what to say, and is reputed strong only because he has remained silent

I cannot pretend to be impartial about the colors. I rejoice with the brilliant ones, and am genuinely sorry for the poor browns

I have never developed indigestion from eating my words

If the human race wishes to have a prolonged and indefinite period of material prosperity, they have only got to behave in a peaceful and helpful way toward one another

We are all worms. But I believe that
I am a glow-worm

Never give in - never, never, never, never, in nothing great or small, large or petty, never give in except to convictions of honor and good sense

73

I'm just preparing my impromptu remarks

74

I like a man who grins when he fights

Healthy citizens are the greatest asset any country can have

Want of foresight, unwillingness to act when action would be simple and effective, lack of clear thinking, confusion of counsel until the emergency comes, until self-preservation strikes its jarring gong - these are the features which constitute the endless repetition of history

No crime is so great as daring to excel

Ending a sentence with a preposition is something up with which I will not put

He has all of the virtues I dislike and none of the vices I admire

It has been said that democracy is the worst form of government except all the others that have been tried

The first quality that is needed is audacity

The problems of victory are more agreeable than those of defeat, but they are no less difficult

My wife and I tried two or three times in the last 40 years to have breakfast together, but it was so disagreeable we had to stop

Politics is the ability to foretell what is going to happen tomorrow, next week, next month and next year. And to have the ability afterwards to explain why it didn't happen

'No comment' is a splendid expression. I am using it again and again

The power of an air force is terrific when there is nothing to oppose it

The power of man has grown in every sphere, except over himself

Politics is almost as exciting as war, and quite as dangerous. In war you can only be killed once, but in politics many times

Nothing can be more abhorrent to democracy than to imprison a person or keep him in prison because he is unpopular. This is really the test of civilization

I always avoid prophesying beforehand, because it is a much better policy to prophesy after the event has already taken place

Battles are won by slaughter and maneuver. The greater the general, the more he contributes in maneuver, the less he demands in slaughter

The reserve of modern assertions is sometimes pushed to extremes, in which the fear of being contradicted leads the writer to strip himself of almost all sense and meaning

93

Sure I am of this, that you have only to endure to conquer

Do not let spacious plans for a new world divert your energies from saving what is left of the old

I am certainly not one of those who need to be prodded. In fact, if anything, I am the prod

Broadly speaking, the short words
are the best, and the old words best
of all

In war as in life, it is often necessary when some cherished scheme has failed, to take up the best alternative open, and if so, it is folly not to work for it with all your might

No idea is so outlandish that it should not be considered with a searching but at the same time a steady eye

For my part, I consider that it will be found much better by all parties to leave the past to history, especially as I propose to write that history myself

I have nothing to offer but blood, toil, tears and sweat

We occasionally stumble over the truth but most of us pick ourselves up and hurry off as if nothing had happened

When you are winning a war almost everything that happens can be claimed to be right and wise

In those days he was wiser than he is now; he used to frequently take my advice

Although prepared for martyrdom,
I preferred that it be postponed